JUST ONE TO A PLUS ONE

Maria Romano

ISBN: 978-0-578-74823-8

DEDICATION

When I started this journey of going from Just One to a plus one, I had pivoted and we know that pivoting happens to be the new buzzword in 2020. I had originally embarked on going out and speaking to Gen Xers and boomers about motivating themselves and getting out of their comfort zone. But that wasn't my passion at the time. I did some soul search and was talking to my sister one day on phone. Telling her about my dilemma and I just didn't think the topic of motiving was going to my drive. My sister Lee said, Maria, you should talk about people finding love again, you're a widow and you were married for many years, you can relate to people that have similar experiences. That would be your wheelhouse. With some soul searching, I did just that. She made me realize I needed to share this with others because you can't google self-education. Because of that conversation, I want to dedicate my book to my sister, Lee Sola for recognizing the purpose and gift I need to share with people. She gave me insight and vision. I love you sissy.

CONTENTS

Dedication

Acknowledgments

Foreword

ACKNOWLEDG-MENTS

This book was a labor love, with tears, and so many emotions. I could not have done this if it wasn't for my coach Thomas Hyde's. He prodded me, coached me, and pushed me out of my comfort zone. Thank you, Thomas, for helping me. At the end of our conversations Thomas would always sign off with "The highest and the best". Thank you for   making me reach higher and get better.

FOREWORD

Have you had this inner dialog with yourself? "I can't believe I'm still alone. I thought I would have found someone by now. What's wrong with me?" The good news is that there is nothing wrong with you. You are probably feeling lonely, but you certainly are not alone. Right now, more people feel isolated and alone than at any other point in recent history. Loneliness is a major problem. It's becoming a bigger problem than the worldwide pandemic. Loneliness can lead to obesity, diabetes, high blood pressure, stroke, heart conditions, depression, and addiction. Maybe you feel hopeless about overcoming your loneliness. Why do you feel hopeless?

The most likely reason you feel hopeless is that you have been lied to about finding love. Most of the programming that you get from movies, television, romance novels, and other literature present the idea that true love is a product of chance. Every single story that you have encountered your entire life has programmed you to believe that love is a product of chance. Take a moment and think about the last movie you watched or romance novel you read. The story probably sounds like the following example. Two people meet each other by accident. They fall in love. There is a misunderstanding and they go their separate ways. But wait that's not the end! By coincidence, they meet again. They kiss, and make-up, and declare their true love for each other. They get married and live happily ever after. It's a great story. But that great story has very little to do with reality. That type of story is a part of our cultural beliefs that reinforce the idea that love only happens by chance.

Love does not only happen by chance. What do I mean by chance? Chance means that you have no control over your destiny when it comes to finding true love. The idea that love happens by chance means you are forced to wait for some random event or coincidence to take place. Do you believe, though, that for generations people have been waiting around for love to come to them? It's simply not true.

For generations, people have felt they had no control over finding love. For many generations, marriages were arranged and individuals had no choice. That feeling of having no control or choice is the reason why you and so many other people feel hopeless when it comes to finding love. You feel hopeless because you are waiting for destiny, fate, or chance to bring love to you. How many times have you heard the phrase, "love will happen when it's going to happen"? That phrase is another example of the lie that love only happens by chance.

The truth is that finding love does not have to be left to chance. The truth is that when it comes to finding true love you have a choice. Instead of having no control over when and where you find love, you get to make decisions that give you control of your love life. You have an opportunity to take steps to ensure that you will find love. Having a choice means you don't have to wait around for coincidence to bring love to your doorstep. You get to be an active participant in bringing love into your life. You actually have more control over your love life than you have ever believed possible. Does that revelation help to erase some of the hopelessness that you feel around finding love? It should, but if it doesn't let me explain more.

If you want success in finding love, you need to understand and believe that everything you have been told about true love is a lie. The fairytales are just not true. Once you believe this, you have your first and most important choice: to take action. All the fairytales and all the stories that created your belief system have encouraged you to do nothing and just wait for Prince or Princess Charming to show up! Your entire life you've been brainwashed to do nothing. However, doing nothing and waiting for coincidence to bring love into your life makes you feel hopeless. You feel hopeless because you have no control. The antidote to feeling to like you have no control is to take action.

Taking action with your love life may be a new concept for you. You may have a fear of taking action. You may be fearful because you don't know where to begin. Maybe you don't feel like you know what to do next. It can be overwhelming.

Every single person that I have coached felt just like you are feeling now. They felt fearful, unsure, and lacked the confidence to attract someone. I felt the same way, too. For me, and every person that I have coached, the fear that we felt dissolved once we understood this a simple concept. The concept is that you can use a process to find love. Using a process may not sound romantic, but the results of using a process will find romance for you.

Let's talk about how using a process worked for you in the past. It's amazing how many people download blueprints, game plans, recipes, and other forms of processes for nearly every single aspect of their lives. When was the last time you did a Google search for the best brownie recipe or best barbeque ribs? The reason you follow a recipe (or a process) is to ensure success in whatever it is you are creating. Rather than reinventing the wheel, people use recipes or blueprints or processes because they guarantee success. People use outlines, recipes, blueprints for unimportant things like making cupcakes, or how to boil an egg without giving it a second thought. Yet most people, because of their societal programming, will not use a process for something as important as finding love.

For over a decade I have performed wedding ceremonies in the wedding capital of the world, Las Vegas, Nevada. I have performed more than 3000 ceremonies and met couples from all over the world. These couples were all ages, all races, cultures, and religions and they all have one commonality; when they chose to find love, they found love. It is from this experience that I have discovered the process of finding love. The process that you will read about in this book has helped many people who were struggling to find love. You will have a deeper understanding of you, what you want, and how to get it. Love can be found when you choose to take action. Taking action will lead you to open yourself (and your heart) to the many opportunities and ways to meet an amazing partner. Don't just leave your love life to chance; learn to live your love life by choice. Now is your time to *Go from a Just One to a Plus One.*

DON'T JUST LIVE YOUR LIFE, LOVE YOUR LIFE!

– Maria Romano

INTRODUCTION

Have you noticed that it seems like there are a lot of people in this world who want to be in a relationship, but they are struggling to find a partner? Or do you feel like nearly everyone around you is in a relationship and you're the only one left single? The truth is that nearly everyone has both experiences. Most people have some time in their life when they are struggling to find a great relationship and some period when they have a great relationship. Is that an accurate description of your relationship experience?

Are you at the point of your life where you are looking for a great relationship? If you are at that point; what does the phrase "great relationship" mean to you? What does a great relationship look like to you? How would you feel in a great relationship? These are probably some really deep questions for you to ponder. In my work, I find that the happy thoughts and feelings of being in a relationship are usually interrupted by a gigantic roadblock. You may have a roadblock smack dab in the middle of your dream of having a wonderful, loving relationship as well. I have also found that most of the roadblocks that people have are self-imposed and easier to dissolve than they think. What is just one of your roadblocks to having a wonderful relationship? Are you too old? Are you too young? Are you not worthy? Is there no one in your town worth dating? People may have different ages, but love is ageless and eternal. Are all of the good ones taken? Let's go ahead and dissolve the last roadblock. All of the good ones are not taken. After all, YOU aren't taken.

The goal of this book is to move you from being just one to being a plus one. What does that mean? You can go from being single to being in a wonderful, supportive, and nurturing relationship. You have the opportunity to open your mind to possibilities in your life that at this moment may seem farfetched or even impossible. Let me assure you that what you think is impossible today can become a reality much faster than you can anticipate. Of course, all great things take time to develop. You have a wonderful opportunity to develop a skill set, game plan, and a roadmap to defining, finding, and creating a wonderful relationship with your choosing. Open your mind to the possibilities of finding a great relationship. That's relatively easy. Your challenge as you read this book is to open your heart to the real possibilities of creating a great relationship. Opening your heart to the possibility of a wonderful, fulfilling relationship is a big challenge, but a challenge with tremendous rewards. Now is the time for you to begin to move from being a just one to a plus one.

Why do you want love? Why do you want to love and to be loved is a question that most people never ask themselves. Why do you think that no one asks the question, "Why do you want love and be loved?" No one asks that question because the desire to love and to be loved is an innate desire that is in nearly every human being on the planet. Loving and being loved is the cornerstone of our survival as human beings. We are physically, mentally, and spiritually wired to be with other people. Think back to the story of Adam and Eve. One of the oldest stories about the first human beings tells of Adam's desire to have a mate. In the story, God creates Eve so that Adam and Eve have companionship. Now some people say everything went downhill from there. Of course, they're joking. When you think about the Adam and Eve story you think about a very personal need to have a human connection. Consider that the worst punishment that's handed down to a prisoner who is already in prison is solitary confinement. Aside from receiving a death penalty, being alone is the worst punishment that a person can receive. Can you imagine being separated from everyone for even a few days? If you are the head of your household it may sound like a blessing and vacation. Can you imagine how you would feel being separated from other people for weeks, months, or years? We go through life communicating and interacting with people nearly every single day. While the world has become simultaneously both closer and distant because of technology, our human need to be close to others and to love and be loved is constant.

The human desire to love and to be loved is more than just an ancient story and some anecdotal evidence. Scientific studies have shown that babies are happier and healthier when they are held. Studies have also shown a direct correlation between people in relationships and life expectancy. If you want to live longer, find a loving partner and you will. If you want to be happier, find a loving partner. If you want to be healthier, find a loving partner. Being in love and having a healthy relationship is shown to improve nearly every aspect of your life. So, don't be surprised if you find yourself desiring a great relationship: it's in your DNA. The key to all of these benefits is finding and creating a loving environment with your partner. Scientific studies have also shown that being in negative, toxic relationships are linked to heart disease, depression, diabetes, and many other illnesses. Need I say more? The process that you will learn in this book will help you to find a loving partner who benefits your life and help you to avoid the partner-challenges that you want to avoid. The foundational process that moves you from being a just one to a plus one is simple to remember but takes time to perfect.

The process is four steps Be Yourself, Love Yourself, Rock Yourself, and Launch Yourself. Let's get started!

ALWAYS BE A FIRST-RATE VERSION OF YOURSELF AND NOT A SECOND-RATE VERSION OF SOMEONE ELSE

– Judy Garland

BE YOURSELF

You are about to learn the first step in the process of going from just one to a plus one. Be yourself! Who are you? How do you describe yourself? Maybe you're thinking, "I know who I am." If you think you know who you are then you probably do. If you feel like you know yourself already, just play along. If you feel like you don't know yourself you will really enjoy this chapter. For many, many years, most of us have worn a lot of different hats and we've taken on different roles. Take a moment and think about the different hats you have worn and the different roles you have played throughout your life. You may have been a mom, a dad, a brother, a sister, a grandparent, or maybe you're an educator, a mechanic, a doctor, or a community leader. You have spent many years being the person that you need to be to fulfill those roles. You have spent many years playing those roles for the people in your life. The time that you spent playing those roles has a way of creating your identity. The identity that you establish because of the roles you play is often created without your permission. Sometimes you fall into a pattern that becomes comfortable. Luckily now you have a choice in creating your own identity. You're at a great time in your life. You're at a time in your life when you can be your authentic self.

Take a moment and think back to when you were younger. I'm talking about the age of 10 or younger when you had the opportunity to maybe be artistic or athletic. Maybe you had the time to build things or read all day or play all day because you didn't have adult responsibilities. Then what happened? You grew up. It's important now at this time in your life to take a hold of yourself and say, "Okay, what do I want to do? Who do I want to be?"

Some of you might be transitioning out of your profession and getting ready to do something really fun that you've been waiting for the right time to do. Maybe your children are out of the house and you are caring for your aging parents and you're ready to find love again. Before you find love again you will benefit greatly by working on being you. When you learn to be yourself, you're going to find somebody that's going to love you for who you are. When is a good time to starting learning to be yourself? Now. Now is the best time! Maybe you are not accustomed to focusing on yourself so it may take time for you to begin the process. You may have given so much of yourself to others that you may need time to learn how to focus on being yourself. A really important concept to keep in mind is that you get to choose who you are. You don't have to be who others say or think you are. Take a moment and write down a few qualities that you want to create within yourself. While you're going through this process take your time and do some soul searching. Once you begin to have a better understanding of who you want to be, you're going to encounter a few dating dirty words.

Past relationships. Do those words send chills down your spine? Let me clue you in on a little secret: Every relationship is not perfect. There is no perfect relationship. There are parts of every relationship that could have been better. We all have residual emotions from our past relationships. We are not immune to conflict and disappointment. Think about your past relationships. Because you're a product of the events and emotions from your past relationships, you may need to do a little inventory. If you were to think back on your previous relationships, what are some of the commonalities? If you were to make a list of the commonalities in your past relationships you should always begin with the same common denominator: you. You are the common denominator in all of your past relationships. You are the common thread in all of your past relationships. You will also be the common thread that connects your past relationships and your future relationships. Do you want to repeat the same mistakes you made in your past relationships when you begin a wonderful new relationship? Do you want to date the same type of partner you chose in your previous relationships? If the answer to those questions is an emphatic NO! then you will have to change. Luckily, it won't be as hard as having your wisdom teeth pulled. I have a process that can help you to change so that you don't fall into the same tired old relationship patterns with the same old unhealthy, toxic partners. The process that I have created is called dysfunctional detoxing. The process takes time and is very eye-opening. Start with these 5 basic questions to begin the dysfunctional detoxing process.

• What did you enjoy about your previous relationship?
• What did you dislike about your previous relationship?
• What was your contribution to the success of your past relationship?
• What was your contribution to the failure of your past relationship?
• What could you have done differently?

Just imagine how much better prepared for your next relationship you would be if you knew the answers to these questions. Like GI Joe said, "Knowing is half the battle". However, I say that knowing is 'just' half the battle. Once you know the answers to these questions you still have to learn how to apply this newfound knowledge to the success of your new relationship. This is the magic of Dysfunctional Detoxifying. Let's take a closer look at how Dysfunctional Detoxifying works considering Anna's experience.

Anna had recently launched her profile on a well-known dating website. She had been on a few dates and then she met somebody she really liked. His name was Terry. His profile looked perfect to Anna. He was divorced, and he was looking for a long-term relationship. They started dating. From there, they moved to the intimacy phase of their relationship. Anna felt that this guy was great for her. She thought things were going well. However, after they moved to the intimacy stage, Terry pulled away from Anna. Terry explained to Anna, "You know, I didn't realize maybe I was rushing too quickly into this relationship." Terry had just recently left a 28-year marriage, and he wanted to slow down. Anna was devastated. Anna was ready to find the perfect person for her, but Terry wasn't ready. He still had residual emotions and emotional baggage from his previous relationship that sabotaged his new relationship with Anna. Do you see why Dysfunctional Detoxing is so very important?

Now, let's change gears. Think about your past relationships. Begin by making a list of what worked really well in your past relationships. (It is helpful to write this down. Grab a notebook and your favorite pen and get cozy!) Did you bring out the best in each other? Were there things that you enhanced about each other? Now begin a new list. What didn't work in your past relationships? What did you do?

What did that other person do? Were there ways that you were at odds with each other?

Did your partner turn out to be a different type of person than you thought they were? Sometimes we meet someone and we like certain traits about them. For example, somebody could be the type of person that spends a lot of time in their career, and you think that's wonderful. However, when you get into a relationship, you begin to be very resentful of the time that they spend working. Next, begin the third list. This list is more difficult than the others because it requires some honest self-reflection. What did YOU do that added to the demise of the relationship? That's right – how did you contribute to the end of the relationship? Think hard and be honest. Relationships and their demise are not one-sided. So, you need to take the time to do some soul searching and think about what role you played. Next, create the fourth list. This list answers a very important question. What could you have done differently to contribute to your previous relation-ships? How could you have acted differently in your past relationships? Next, make the fifth list. This is a master list. On your master list write down the qualities and traits from your first four lists that you want in your next relationship. This master list is the one that you can use to begin creating a deeper understanding of what you want in your next rela-tionship. Think of this master list as a roadmap to the first step of the just one to plus one process; be yourself.

TO FALL IN LOVE WITH YOURSELF IS THE FIRST SECRET TO HAPPINESS

– Robert Morley

LOVE YOURSELF

A s you learn more about who you are through the be yourself process, you get the wonderful opportunity to love yourself. This is my favorite part but it is often the hardest part to master. But first, let's take a moment and reflect. You went through the different roles that you played in your life. And then you also looked at the different relationships you've had in your life, and then you began working on getting rid of the residual feelings of your past relationships through the process of dysfunctional detoxing. You may be thinking that you've got a better understanding of who you are. Maybe you would assume that loving yourself is easy. It isn't that easy. We are our own worst critics Let me give you a couple of analogies here. I want you to think about somebody in your life that you love.

Take a moment and close your eyes. Visualize that person. Smell them. Feel them. Now open your eyes. What did you see? You really didn't see that physical person. You might have seen their smile, their eyes, but what you saw was the beautiful attributes and the emotions that they exude with their personality. You probably remembered the way they made you feel. Maybe there's somebody in your life whose smile you just love. Or maybe it's the way somebody gets a look in their eyes. It's very inviting and very trusting when we start to think of other people, their characteristics and qualities. However, most people place quite a bit of emphasis on how they look. But do you know what? You are not a size. You are not an age. You're not a financial report. You are a beautiful creation. Have you heard your friends say things like they are not young enough, rich enough, or thin enough to date? Being young enough, rich enough, or thin enough is not a requirement for love. Those traits are certainly not requirements for loving yourself. It's important to remember that you are unique and that there is no-body in the world like you. That's right. Nobody else in the world has your DNA. What's unique is valuable. What's rare is valuable. You are unique and rare. You are valuable. You are certainly worthy of love.

It's time to do some more writing. Create a list entitled, 'love myself.' On this list write down three things that you like about you. Write down three things that you love about you. Then, ask some of your friends to write down three things that they love about YOU. Find out how wonderful the people around you think you are. Your friends may tell you they love your smile or that your warm per-sonality makes people feel like they can trust you.

Maybe they love the way that you are the life of the party or that they can always depend on you to be there in times of trouble. Once you get a few lists from your friends combine those with the list that you created. This love list is a great way to remind yourself why you should love yourself as much as you can. Memorize this list. Put a copy in your wallet. Put a copy on your bathroom mirror. There will be days in your future when you will be glad that you did.

Now create another list. This list should be titled, 'improve myself.'   Begin to list what you can do to improve yourself. Your list may include; Be more loving, be more patient, be more assertive. This list requires action. For each of the items that you list create a why and a how. These are your reasons for improvement and your method for improvement. When should you start improving yourself? Now. Now is the time to work on you. Now's the time to be the best version of you.

If being the best includes focusing on your outward appearance, that is fine. If you need to lose weight start now. Don't put it off. Lose the weight if you need to not because you want to be the same weight as you were in your 20's. That's probably not realistic. I tell my clients, "Healthy looks great on everyone". So, focus on healthy weight and not being too thin. I also recommend working on your teeth before you spend money on Botox, fillers, injections, or a facelift. Your teeth say everything about your health. Start with your smile and if you want to work on any other part of yourself do so. However, remember before you have any type of surgery to improve yourself physically you must make sure your positive internal qualities have a chance to shine.

Let's take a moment and reflect on what you wrote and what you think about yourself. Let me tell you why. When you get into the dating arena, you're going to get your ass kicked. It is not always easy and you need to make sure you have the right tools to help you when you get knocked down so that you can pick yourself up. You need to focus on the great qualities you have and what you have to offer. You are not going to be all things to all people. Let me say this again because it is so important: You are not going to be all things to all people. Here's a great example of that. When my husband and I started our rental car company in 1979, I went out to all the bellmen in Las Vegas because they were a great source of referrals. I'll never forget when my husband, Frank, gave me a stack of $5.00 bills to give to each of the bellmen for their first rental referral. Most Bell Captains were thrilled, however, there were a couple that would not take the first referral fee. I could not understand why they wouldn't take the money. Frank gave me some sage advice. He said, "A good salesperson is paid for their no's." It took me many years to fully understand that and this is the same analogy for dating. You will have rejection, but when you find the right one for you the payoff is PRICELESS. Take the time to you nurture yourself. Shield yourself from the negative and amplify the positive.

SEVEN DAYS OF LOVING YOURSELF

Loving yourself is both a state being and a practice. The state of being is supported by daily practice. A concert pianist sits down confidently to play a concerto because she has spent years practicing. Loving yourself works the same way. Loving yourself will be much easier when you devote yourself to daily practice. Here's a week's worth of loving yourself practice that you can implement.

Day 1. Self-Compassion.
Day 2. Compliment yourself.
Day 3. Self-Forgiveness.
Day 4. Focus on your health.
Day 5. Feed your mind.
Day 6. Feed your spirit.
Day 7. Rest and Relax.

Day 1. Self-Compassion is a gateway into the other days that follow. Self-Compassion is a three-step process. Firstly, very simply, be as kind, gentle, and understanding with yourself as you would be with someone you care about. Secondly, remember that you are not alone in the world. Other people have the same problems and have made the same mistakes. Thirdly, observe yourself and the world around you without judgment. These three steps in the self-compassion process will help you to combat the anxiety, depression, and low self-esteem that make it nearly impossible to feel great and find love.

Day 2. Give yourself compliments throughout the day to acknowledge how wonderful you are. Don't wait for someone else to give you compliments. Give them to yourself. Say them aloud. You need to hear you giving yourself compliments. The world is a hypercritical place. You need the added boost. Be generous with the compliments! Self-criticism is not a great motivator and often leads to low energy and anxiety.

Day 3. Self-Forgiveness is a deliberate decision to let go of the feelings of anger, resentment, and revenge that you have directed towards yourself.

Day 4. Focus on your health. This can mean a lot of things for you. You can get a massage or visit the chiropractor. Maybe you will go for a long walk or take a yoga class. Maybe you can take this day to eat healthy meals that you enjoy or to get in some long-overdue exercise. Remember that healthy looks good on everybody.

Day 5. Feeding your mind sounds like something all busy adults need. This day is about giving your mind a chance to relax and allowing you to dream. This is the day that you can move from all the daily tasks that wear away at you and allow your imagination to be set free. If you are typically under stimulated mentally, then maybe this is a day for you to do something that stimulates your mind. Either way, take care of your mental health today.

Day 6. Feeding your spirit is a very individual practice. I use the term spirit and soul interchangeably. What soothes your spirit? How do you care for your soul? Maybe you meditate or pray on this day. Maybe you play music or paint. Take this day to feed the invisible you.

Day 7. Resting and relaxing is easier said than done. I have seen many personal schedules and never once seen rest and relax penciled into a time slot. In this often-busy world, you have to schedule and prioritize relaxation. You will find that loving yourself is much easier when you are well-rested.

So much of this advice is truly common sense. Unfortunately, common sense advice usually gets thrown out the window when you find yourself bombarded by family obligations, deadlines at work, and all of the boring, repetitive tasks of life. Loving yourself will require action, practice, and repetition. I have another little secret for you. When you get into that dating arena, you're likely to meet people who are going to attempt to shatter your confidence. Some people do it unintentionally. Some do it intentionally. You might go out on a date with someone who you think is wonderful and then they ghost you. Maybe you never hear from them again. What if they say, "Listen, I think you're great, but you just don't look exactly like your pictures"? That can be a major blow to your ego and challenge your self-love. Let me share Susan's story with you. Susan is in her early sixties. She's an educated brunette who was looking to find love. Susan took my course and she met someone online. His name was Sal and he was about 12 years younger than Susan. Susan and Sal met for a drink and she wasn't too sure she liked him. Sal just kept talking about how great he was, what he had accomplished, and the people he knows. (On a side note: Ladies and Gentlemen, please do not recite your resume. You are at an age in life and have so much experience that you know someone should not have to give you a hard sell). Susan and Sal parted ways and never talked about meeting again. Well, Sal texted her later that night and asked if she wanted to come over, get in the hot tub, have some champagne, and have sex. Susan was flabbergasted. She sent him a note and told him he was a great guy but not a match for her. Sal texted her back and said, "I wasn't really interested in you. You're too bottom-heavy for me anyway." Wow! Can you believe that? Susan could have fixated on what Sal said but she understood his ego was bruised. Remember, you will have rejection but always focus on loving yourself. When negative thoughts occur, you can push them aside and give yourself those compliments. These are the times when loving yourself will save your self-confidence.

I have one little suggestion to share with you that has helped me when I've had times where my self-confidence was challenged. Listen to commencement speeches. Most of the best commencement speeches are written by people that have some life experience and perspective. They usually have great tips about how to handle life. These speeches can make you feel motivated and magnificent. If you want to try something more active you can crank up some happy, uplifting music and start dancing and singing. You can sing and dance like no-one is watching or listening. Now, don't put on a depressing break-up song. Put on something that's going to make you happy and just dance and sing. Find a physical way to rid yourself of those negative feelings that injure your self-confidence so that you can get back to loving yourself. You deserve it.

Never bend your head. Always hold it up and high. Look someone straight in the eye

– HELEN KELLER

ROCK YOURSELF

So now let's move on to Rock Yourself. To rock yourself is to proudly display who you are to the world. When you rock yourself, you are feeling free enough to express yourself. You let the real you be seen by the rest of the world. That's right, rock yourself. Love the skin you're in. Love yourself from roots to boots. Today is the day. When you step into your shoes, you show off like a proud peacock spreading those feathers. No feather on a peacock is alike. Just like you. You're unique. Have you ever seen the movie, 'I Feel Pretty' starring Amy Schumer? Amy Schumer plays a woman who is in her late 30s. She is overweight. She's been constantly overlooked for promotion in her career and she's still looking for the love of her life. So she decides to take charge of her life. She goes to the gym. She takes a cycle class. She gets on a bicycle. She falls off the bicycle and hits her head. She wakes up in a hospital and has a concussion, but when she wakes up, she thinks she's a supermodel. Now, remember, she hasn't changed. She still looks the same as she did before the concussion, but her belief about how she looks has changed. Because she's looking in the mirror and she is seeing a version of herself as a superstar supermodel, she goes out in the world and she gets the dream job that she wants. And she also finds the love of her life. She never lost a pound. Why was she so successful? Because she made that one little adjustment within herself by being confident. Being confident is what rocking yourself is all about. You will have a much happier and successful life as you become more confident with who you are. Learning how to rock yourself can take a long time, but we're going to take a few shortcuts.

Here's a game plan for you. Visualize yourself wearing an outfit that makes you feel like a king or a queen. Imagine that you feel free and confident. Visualize yourself going through your day with all of the confidence that you feel in your visualization. Every day when you get up, imagine that outfit on you. Don't let your feelings about yourself dictate your visualization. Visualize that outfit every morning and emotionally connect to how you feel in your visualization. When you begin to use this visualization, you will see that the image you visualize will become clearer. That picture of yourself will become more vivid and realistic. As the clarity of your visualization improves, your self-esteem will also improve. When you rock yourself and you know who you are, you're going to attract somebody that's going to rock you. Then you're going to rock each other's world! When you get into that dating arena, you're going to have a lot of different experiences. Some of your experiences are going to be very positive. Some of them are going to be negative. Again, you're trying to keep your self-esteem and self-confidence safeguarded against these negative experiences.

Sometimes rocking yourself is a serious challenge. Think about a time in your life when you've walked into a situation where you felt uncomfortable. Did you feel like you were lacking self-confidence? Maybe you felt uncomfortable when you walked into the gym because you weren't as fit as everybody else. Perhaps you attended a meeting within your profession and felt like you were not good enough or smart enough. Here's a little secret: no one else was thinking that about you, but a lot of people were thinking that about themselves. You control your thoughts. When you have those thoughts or insecurities, remember they come from you and no one else. Make the choice today to stop feeling uncomfortable. Just like the movie "I feel pretty" with Amy Schumer, commit to telling yourself that you're confident.

I had a light bulb moment that may help you, too. I was listening to a talk given by Maya Angelou. She said, "When you are going into a situation where you feel uncomfortable or insecure, you can take your tribe with you". Your tribe is the collection of people in your life, both past and present, that are your biggest cheerleaders. Imagine them surrounding you as you enter that situation. I like to call this your Love Tribe. Start to build up your Love Tribe. As you surround yourself with your love tribe you will create a charismatic aura around you. The people around you will notice the change in your confidence and your charisma. You will be magnetic. Visualize your Love Tribe.

SEVEN DAYS OF ROCKING YOURSELF

Here are seven simple but powerful affirmations that will help you be confident and help you step into your personal power each and every day. Say these aloud to help you Rock Yourself

• I am and always will be enough. Remember you are enough. You are a masterpiece.

• I am courageous. You are willing to act and face your fears. Remember, you have nothing to fear but fear itself. So, go forward with your life. Be courageous!

• I release the old negative beliefs that have stood in the way of my success. We tend to hold on to negative beliefs that have held us back. Shed those beliefs. That's right, just forget about them. When you think about them, eliminate those thoughts and move forward.

- Feeling confident is a normal part of my everyday life. You can always bring your love tribe with you any time you need a confidence boost.

- I am energetic and enthusiastic. You bring increased energy and excitement to every positive part of your life.

- My mind is clear of self-doubt. Every day you're going to have opportunities before you. Take advantage of them. Enjoy them.

- I make decisions based on the superstar I am. You are a superstar. Trust your instincts and decision making.

You're ready to take on the world! It's going to be challenging at times, however, the rewards you will reap from rocking yourself will be greater than you can imagine. It's going to take you time, effort, and commitment to show the new you to the world. It's a big part of the process of finding true love in your life. Rock yourself so that you can move from being a just one to a plus one.

GET COMFORTABLE BEING UNCOMFORTABLE

LAUNCH YOURSELF

I n the work that I do, I find that most of my new clients are focused on how their online dating profile looks. They're concerned with how much attention their profile is getting or not getting. They often feel as if they only had the perfect profile then they could find the perfect person for them. That just isn't the case. Learning about yourself puts you into the position to take the next step. Congratulations! You've already done the work. The preparatory work of learning to Be yourself, Love Yourself, and Rock Yourself prepares you for the next step: Launch Yourself. Launching yourself is you announcing to the world that you are wonderful and available.

Why do you need to launch yourself? If you were looking for a new job would you be standing out on the sidewalk with a sandwich board? Probably not. So why would you do the online equivalent of standing on a street corner with a sandwich board in your search for a loving relationship? To find a loving relationship you can follow a business model that has years of proven success. You can both brand yourself and market yourself. By branding and marketing yourself, you can position yourself to become a very valuable commodity and fast track your way to a loving relationship.

Much like a pilot, you wouldn't take off down the runway and plan to read the "How to pilot an airplane plane" book once you were in the air. Launching yourself is much more than just putting a dating app profile and pictures online. Launching yourself is really about announcing yourself to the world. To begin the launch yourself process you will begin with branding. Let's start with the visuals. Not your online pictures, but rather the visualization of what your relationship looks like. Notice that I didn't say what your partner will look like. I said what your relationship looks like. When most people are asked to describe their perfect partner, they have a list of criteria. Ask the average guy on the street and he may say 5'7" tall, blonde, blue eyes and long legs. While that may be the partner he is looking for, those criteria don't directly translate into a successful relationship. The criteria that we want to focus on is this—How does your partner make you feel in your relationship? That is a very big question. How does your future partner make you feel? Can you list some of the feelings you want to have when you are in your perfect relationship?

I challenge you to pull out that notebook again

and choose five feelings that you want to feel and write them down. The five feelings will come in very handy in your next step. The next step after writing down the feelings that you want to feel in a relationship is to find images that represent those feelings to you. Find images that both evoke and inspire those feelings within you. Once you've found those images it's time to create a vision board. A vision board is the physical representation of visualization. Think of it as the physical focus and clarity of what you want in a relationship. This physical focus and clarity are the branding of you and the relationship that you want. The vision board is a great way for you to keep your eye on the prize of an amazing relationship. As we mature, we recognize that it's more important to have someone who makes you feel good than someone who just looks good. The vision board is a physical system of checks and balances to keep you focused on what's important - how you feel. It's a great tool for accountability. The vision board will keep you on a clear path when you find yourself experiencing some of the hiccups that are bound to occur when you begin dating.

The first rule of the vision board is this. It's not enough to know that you should make a vision board. You have to make your vision board. A few of the qualities of a vision board should be that it is simple, direct, uncluttered, and inspirational. Think about the vision board as your personal brand. Can you imagine the Nike symbol? It's just a swoosh, but millions of people around the world think of that swoosh as the phrase, 'just do it.' The images on your vision board represent the brand image of your relationship. Ensure that the images you choose are evocative and direct. Rather than cluttering your mind with many different images, just pick a few. Pick images that evoke emotions within you that you would like to feel when you are in love. Then, place your vision board in a place where you can see it daily. Some of my clients keep their vision boards on their desks. Some of them keep them in the kitchen. One of my clients put her vision board in front of her bathroom mirror so that she can see it first thing in the morning even before she brushes her teeth. What a way to start your morning!

Now that you have a brand image for your relationship it's time to create a brand image for you. We have already spent time focusing on uncovering the authentic person who you are. Now we need to make sure that the images, words, and persona that you portray are realistic and match the authentic you. Let's start with the photos that you choose for your online profile. A picture is worth 1000 words. You're probably tired of hearing it and I'm tired of saying it. How you portray yourself with your pictures is paramount to attracting the right attention that you want. In general, selfies are not flattering. They can often be the most unflattering picture you can post depending upon the angle. If you're going to post a selfie, I suggest you use a selfie stick. It really makes for a better photo. Excellent lighting can improve the quality of any photograph that you take. YouTube has many videos on how you can set up a beautiful photo by using simple lighting techniques.

To create an online profile, you need four great photos. These photos should be in alignment with your personal brand. You need one headshot, one full body shot, and two pictures of you being active. The photos are likely to represent the authentic you very well. While most people have a cell phone with an amazing camera, photos are best left to the professionals. For very little money you can have a professional photographer take your photos and make you shine. Remember to choose flattering colors, outfits, and natural poses. You don't want your photos to look like 1970's Olan Mills photos. Please only post pictures of yourself, not your animals, your friends, your family, or your children. Focus on you. You are promoting your brand which is you!

Let's talk about writing your online profile. Your online profile is a part of your marketing. I always assist my clients in creating their profiles. Your profile is too important to leave to chance. I recommend that you get professional assistance from someone who will take the time to know and understand you. With a little insightful, empathetic assistance you can create an authentic profile. Let's talk through a few guidelines to help you if you decide to write your own profile. You want to be able to describe yourself in about three paragraphs. Any more than three paragraphs and you're going to lose people. I can't begin to tell you how many people write a book for a profile. If you write a book-length profile people will wonder what's wrong with you. Begin your profile with something positive about you and something that you love. Do not begin your profile with something negative about you or one of your negative preferences. Negativity tends to attract negative people. You probably have enough problems already the last thing you need is negative people 'hitting you up.' How many times have you seen a profile which begins with, "I don't want any drama"?

Those are often the profiles of negative people who are constantly surrounding themselves with dramatic people, situations, and events. Starting your profile with your political preferences or your religious preferences is not ideal. Both of these are real hot buttons for people and you may find yourself being harassed by someone who isn't really looking at you as a potential partner. They may have just noticed the first sentence of your profile and couldn't help but disagree with your beliefs, often in a childish and hurtful manner. Feel free to express your religious and political beliefs a little farther into your profile. You may not want to describe yourself as a couch potato. Couch potato. That doesn't sound very attractive, does it?

Do let potential suitors know that you are interested in an LTR. A long-term relationship. Some of my clients will object to this part because they think it will limit their pool of potential dates. I tell them, "Yes. You're right!"   The point is that there are more than enough people to choose from and you have to narrow your audience. You don't want to end up with someone who is a serial dater while you're expecting to create a long-lasting relationship. Take a few sentences to highlight the areas of your life that are important to you on your profile. You can spend time talking about what you appreciate such as family, friendship, faith, hobbies, and travel. Put effort and intelligence into creating your profile and it will be a reflection of your personal brand.

Your profile should be listed on more than one dating site. To begin with, I recommend two. If you are newly returning to the dating world, two dating apps are a lot to juggle. There are so many dating apps available right now. Take your time and do some research on the apps. You want to find an app that is in alignment with your goals. I strongly recommend that you place your profile on a dating app that asks you a multitude of questions. The more questions the app asks you, the more effectively the algorithms can match you up with somebody who is a good match for you! Those apps that don't ask you many questions typically do very little to help you weed out poor matches. So take the time to place yourself on at least two dating apps. I recommend that you choose a dating app that is fee-based. Typically, free apps will give you exactly what you pay for them.

When you do find the apps that you want to use go ahead and upload your profile and pictures. You may be thinking you're happy that you're all done. Not so fast. Now you get the wonderful opportunity to begin browsing other people's profiles. Don't wait for somebody to reach out to you. Reach out to them. Once you launch yourself online check your dating apps once in the morning and once in the evening. Resist the urge to spend all day looking at your apps. Spend some time browsing profiles and making comments. Refrain from just leaving a like or an emoji. Take the time to ask a creative question to learn more about a person you are interested in. This kind of response lets someone know that you are creative, intelligent, interested, and present. This is what someone who is committed to finding the perfect person for themselves would do. You will definitely get more attention from someone you're interested in because people are often flattered when you bother to read their entire profile.

I recommend exchanging messages through the dating app first. Then when you're ready to move your communication from online to offline you may choose to exchange telephone numbers. If somebody is long-distance maybe you can use Face-Time or Zoom video. You can use online video chat services before you meet in person or exchange phone numbers. This is a great option for you if you are uncomfortable with the dating process. This is the process that I recommend for all of my clients. Let your first date be a virtual date. You can connect with your date over the online chat services like Skype or Zoom and learn quite a lot about your date before you meet them in person. It's a great way to safely meet and greet and to save time. Then you will feel more comfortable when you meet IRL (In Real Life). What's great about the exposure on these dating apps is that you're getting to meet people from all over the world and you never know where you can find Mr. or Mrs. Right. They can be in your backyard or they can be across the seas. This is the time of your life where you can open up your world and meet people from different races, cultures, religions, and maybe even political preferences. If James Carville and Mary Matalin are life-long partners and married since 1993 maybe you can do the same as well.

Below you will find a list of red flags. Sometimes we get so caught up in the moment of online dating that we are falling in love with a false concept of who a person is based on their profile. These Red Flags will help you avoid them.

- Anyone that asks you for money

- Pictures look too good to be real

- When the person exchanges emails or texts

you after which they go into a sob story.

•　An individual who feels that work is against him or her.

•　The person only talks about how great they are. Narcissistic personality.

•　Does not listen to the exchange of dialogue either over the phone or in person. Listening skills are so important.

•　Someone who wants to move from A to Z immediately. Anyone that pressures you for either intimacy or exclusivity after one or two dates. When you jump into a relationship quickly the opposite can occur and you can also jump out as well.

•　A person avoids calling just wants to text or email.

•　Someone that does not want to show their picture (Could indicate they are in a committed relationship)

I always tell my clients to not look at the online dating apps as the cure-all and as the only solution to attracting the perfect person for you. There are other pathways to finding true love. First, let's take a look at a not-so-obvious pathway. One thing that you can do is announce to all of your friends, family, and coworkers that you're looking to find love. Feel free to do this repeatedly. Let them know that you're out there in the dating world. Ask them, "Hey, if you know somebody that you think might be a good fit might be a good match for me, please let me know." They can give you their contact information and you can begin to communicate. Some people are hesitant to help because they don't like playing matchmaker and some are going to just love playing the matchmaker.

Let's not forget the very best way of marketing you in the dating world. Word of mouth advertising is the oldest form of marketing and it is still viable. Let's work off of a referral. What better way to do business? Over the past decade, I have married many couples that met through friends. Some people have been introduced by their butcher, their baker, or their real estate agent. One couple whose ceremony I performed met through her hairdresser. So, word of mouth is a great way to start the process. You can also take action by going to Meetups, church functions, sports activities, and community events. If you're a little shy contact the host of the event before you attend and tell them that you are new and ask them if they can provide some assistance. Put yourself out there. The best way to advertise yourself is by You.

STEP OUT OF YOUR COMFORT ZONE

THE FIRST DATE

The first date is a subject that perplexes and worries some of my clients. Even after learning all about themselves and having a successful launch and finding a great prospect, they agonize over the first date. There is an internal journey that happens when you are in this stage of your dating process. You've put in a lot of hard work. You may find that there is a barrier to taking the next step. The roadblock to the first meet and greet is often the same for most of my clients. The big roadblock is fear. Fear is the number one reason why some people have a really hard time moving from the sidelines and on to the dating field. If you find that you are repeatedly getting stuck when the next step is to meet someone, you may be manipulated by fear. Fortunately, people often overcome their fear of the first meeting by learning some of the simple rules for a first date.

I agree with Dwight D. Eisenhower who said, "I have always found that plans are useless, but planning is indispensable." There is no winging it on the planning of your first date. The first date should be planned spontaneity. That means there should be a sound firm structure that supports your ability to be carefree. This may sound contradictory now, but it should make sense to you in just a minute. The first date should have two components that can ensure your date is enjoyable even if you don't make a love connection. Safety and Fun.

Maybe you're wondering why you should begin with safety first. Unless you are an extreme thrill seeker you will probably enjoy a roller coaster ride more with the safety equipment on than with no safety equipment at all. Safety in the dating world is characterized by boundaries. The boundaries that you will set are a pathway to freedom. I know that may seem unlikely, but let me explain. If you set very specific safety boundaries for your first meeting you can ensure that you can relax and have fun because you are not in any perceived danger. As my friend Thomas likes to say, "It's really hard to enjoy a good whiskey during a gunfight." At the same time, it's really difficult to engage in meaningful conversation when you're preoccupied with your safety. Do you think it would be possible to have a wonderful time while you're afraid that your date may kidnap you halfway through coffee? By utilizing these safety precautions, you can also learn more about the person who you will be meeting for the first time. For example, if your date insists that you meet in a remote location it's an immediate red flag. Anyone with good intentions understands that safety ensures that you both can enjoy a great first date.

The first rule of safe dating is location. Location. Location. It's not just important in real estate it's vitally important to safety on a first date. The location that you should choose to meet on a first date should have several qualities. Firstly, it must be public. No meeting in a private or remote area. Ten adults go missing every day in the United States and you don't want to be one of them. Stay safe by meeting in a public place such as a restaurant, coffee shop, or museum.

Secondly, arrive alive and leave happy. To ensure that a would-be suitor doesn't learn where you live and work too early, be sure to take your own transportation to and from the desired meeting location. I have been told by my clients that in the past they were offered rides on a first date. This is a No-No. If someone insists that you get in a vehicle with them it is a huge red flag that at the very least, they have boundary issues, and quite possibly they may intend to do you harm. If you don't have your own vehicle be sure to utilize a ride share service or taxi cab. Don't accept a ride from anyone no matter how comfortable you feel on a first date.

Thirdly, get an accountability buddy. Be sure that someone you trust knows these three facts about your date. Let your buddy know where you're going, what time you are going, and have them expect a phone call from you when you're done. This, of course, means that at the end of the date when you are safely at home you should call your accountability buddy to let them know that you are safe.

Fourth, leave them wanting more! As tempting as it may be to spend hours or even days with your first date, it's a really bad idea. Just like in show business, you always want to leave them wanting more. Spend about 30 minutes to 1 hour on the first few dates. These first dates are really an opportunity to rely on your intuition and to have some fun without getting too comfortable. What do I mean by that? It's really easy to let your guard down with someone when you are spending a long time with them. If the first few dates are long you may create an artificial trust between you two that is built on a false sense of security. I recommend telling your date-to-be these few easy sentences. "Even though I only have a short amount of time, I'm looking forward to meeting you in person. Can you meet for 30 minutes to an hour on Saturday at 2?" This will ensure that you have set some very valuable time boundaries. Remember if you spend too much time with someone you may seem needy or desperate for attention. Once you have the safety measures in place for your first date it's time for you to have fun!

Your date should revolve around activity and conversation. The activity should be something that you both can enjoy. Maybe that's coffee, lunch, or ice skating. Be sure that the activity is fun, but not so distracting that you don't get to know one another.

Remember, the first rule of dating conversation is to always be polite. If everything else about your screening process is great, then you should be able to have a pleasant conversation with your first date. On your first date, you want to be sure that you keep the conversation relatively light and not too intrusive. I like to share these guidelines for first date conversations with my clients.

These are some topics you can discuss during your first meet and greet
- What is exciting in your life?
- Where did you grow up? Tell me more about that.
- Tell me about your perfect vacation. What did you like the best and why?
- Do you have any children? Grandchildren?
- Do you have any hobbies?
- Tell me something about you.

These are some topics you should avoid during your first meet and greet
- Past relationships
- Income
- Any negative topics

Attempt to change the subject if your date brings up these topics
- Past relationships
- Any past trauma (this can be discussed the more you two get to know one another)

- Shopping for wedding rings.

Here are a few Red Flags to watch out for on your first date.

- They only talk about how great they are. This may be the sign of someone selfish, insecure, conceited, or narcissistic.
- Does not listen to the exchange of dialogue either over the phone or in person. Listening skills are so important
- Someone who wants to move from A to Z immediately. Anyone that pressures you for either intimacy or exclusivity after one or two dates.

When you jump into a relationship quickly the opposite can occur and you can also jump out as well. Dating conversations should be fun and light-hearted. Neither of you should be questioning the other like an investigative journalist. Don't bombard your date with questions and don't ramble on about yourself or your cat. Have a great first date!

LIFE IS LIKE BEING
ON A TRAIN YOU
DON'T KNOW
ALL STOPS AS
WELL AS WHERE
PEOPLE IN LIFE
GET ON AND
OFF THE TRAIN

DATING A WIDOW OR WIDOWER

One of the big challenges that face you when you're dating as an adult is dating someone who has been widowed. Having a relationship with someone who has lost a significant other is a little different than dating someone who is divorced or recently has left a relationship. When someone is divorced the other partner may still be a part of their life. Often, a divorced couple may still share children, assets, or relationships. However, with death, it is completely different. It's different because that person would not be out in the dating world again had they not lost their partner. They would have still been with their partner.

Being a widow myself, I became acutely aware of the situation as it pertains to dating. Here are a few tips. I tell clients that are dating someone who has lost their spouse to always be compassionate and empathetic about the deceased. Always. It's very important because your partner will almost assuredly take offense to anything negative that you may say about their former partner. It's much better to be mindful of someone who has passed away. Often a partner may have children from the previous relationship. Refrain from badmouthing your partner's ex, it's a sure-fire way to distance yourself from your partner and their children. The deceased spouse who is no longer in their life is still someone very significant, even to the person that you're dating. Sometimes your partner may want to share stories about the person that they lost. I suggest that you not take that personally? Also, you should not be offended? Maybe they're just sharing a little bit about their life. Their life may have been deeply rooted in their relationship with their former partner.

As time goes on you will create history, develop experiences, and share memories together. Over time the subject of the deceased partner typically lessens and their stories will revolve around your shared experiences. Just remember to never speak ill, no matter what, about the person that passed away.

There is a special circumstance that I want to highlight for you that can be a real relationship destroying trap. There may be times in your relationship when your partner makes a negative comment about their late partner. Do not fall into the trap. This is not the time for you to agree or make any comment. I suggest that you just nod your head and listen? If the person that you're dating asks you something like, "Don't you think my ex was wrong or inconsiderate," take a neutral position. Be like Switzerland. Stay neutral. This can be tough but just hold back. If you feel compelled to speak you can say, "I really don't know both sides and I would rather not comment." Just allow that person you're with the room to talk about them. Don't change the subject. It may seem like an uncomfortable situation, but typically there is nothing unnatural about the conversation. The attitude of making comments about some's deceased spouse is very detrimental, let me share with you how that creates havoc in your new relationship. Jennifer was a widow and she had recently begun dating a new guy named Jack. Jennifer found herself recounting several stories about her previous relationship with Jack. Some of Jennifer's stories had given Jack a little perspective about her former spouse, or so he thought. Jack had heard enough stories about Jennifer's former spouse that he felt compelled to comment about her Ex. Jack said, "Well it sounds like he just wasn't a very nice man, your late husband." Jennifer was taken aback. Jennifer asked, "What made you say that?" Jack said, "Just based upon the experiences that you said you had with him." She said, "I never gave you any indication that he wasn't a good husband. I think you're misconstruing what I'm saying." This conversation was a real point of contention between Jennifer and Jack. Instead of letting the conversation become a point of contention, allow the conversation to be a pathway for your partner to move on with their life. Often these conversations are your partner's ways of opening up their world to you. It's a very vulnerable conversation.

Allow the conversations to enlighten you about your partner and their past. Needless to say, but if a person you're dating is constantly talking about their deceased spouse, that's a different story. If the conversation is constantly about the deceased ex-partner you may need to take a different action. Obviously, this is your decision. Please tread lightly. You may recommend grief counseling for your spouse. Again, now is the time to be gentle and understanding. Grief counseling or professional therapy can be an amazing tool to help someone you care about move past their sorrow and grief. Sometimes your partner may be experiencing survivor's guilt. The guilt of living after your partner has passed on can be devastating. Sometimes that guilt may continue because they are moving on with YOU. Your partner may even feel like they are cheating on their Ex or their Ex's memory. That's quite common.

Very early on in my dating experiences after my husband died, I met a gentleman who was widowed after 50 years of marriage. His wife had passed away three years earlier and my husband had passed away just two years earlier. You would have been intrigued by our early conversations while we were dating. He always spoke of his late wife as if she was there. I mean he spoke of her as if she were in the room with us. He had major conflicts with dating after she passed away. He felt that he needed to keep memorializing her. As a result, there was some conflict between us. In hindsight, we could have been more patient and understanding with each other. A few months after we stopped dating, he reached out and told me he realized that maybe he needed more time to heal. He felt that he had jumped back into the dating world too soon. Although he was a widow at that time for almost three years, he still needed resolution. Just because a certain amount of time has passed doesn't mean that you are ready to date after you have lost someone you love.

So always be mindful never to say anything negative about someone whose spouse/significant other passed away. Remember that in time, as you develop a history together, you're going to be talking about the experiences that you share. Be compassionate. Be present. What do you think will happen? What will happen is they will develop a strong personal bond with you in time. As time goes by, you'll have a happy with a healthy relationship. Give the person you're dating the grace to talk about their beloved that passed away. As your relationship blossoms, the two of you will be moving together to become a couple. You two will then start developing your story together.

I CAN'T CHANGE
THE DIRECTION
OF THE WIND,
BUT I CAN ADJUST
MY SAILS TO
ALWAYS REACH
MY DESTINATION

– Jimmy Dean

DATING A P.E.S; PROFESSIONAL, ENTREPRENEUR OR SELF EMPLOYED

I have many clients who are winding down their careers and if they meet someone busy in their profession, they pass, they move on. However, if you meet someone and you think you have the possibility of having a great relationship, read on for insight on what to expect and how to create a relationship.

You met someone who has a career or they just started a new business or have an existing one. You might have just started a relationship or are about to and you're not too sure where you fit in. It can be a little frustrating and almost a competition as to who gets the most attention. It can be the equivalent to a third person in a relationship.

When you are starting a new relationship and someone has their own business or they are in an important position at a company where they have a large number of responsibilities, it could cause problems. You both want to become exclusive and want to spend more time together. Be direct and honest and just ask, "Will you have enough time for us to spend together?"

When someone is interested, even with other responsibilities they will make time to have a successful relationship. However, the person who isn't as busy with their life also needs to be flexible. If this someone you want in your life long term, you can be flexible. That is what it takes to have a strong foundation with good communication and commitment to each other.

The other approach with this new relationship is that you can try to fight for attention. That won't get you very far in the relationship. It's a no-win situation. Someone's livelihood should never be challenged when it comes to a new relationship. Even if you are in a long term one, too.

The person you are dating has spent many years and maybe invested a lot of money and time to get where they are today. And that maybe what attracted you to him or her. However, you both are at a stage where you are not starting as a young couple - more than likely you are 40 and beyond.

Although competing with a business can be difficult, you need to try to understand what the other person may be experiencing. Maybe they just received a promotion in their company, and he or she may want to make sure they are giving their time and learning all the different moving parts as well as working with new people or a new team. That can be unsettling – have a little understanding of what they are experiencing. Or the person you're dating owns a company or just started one. He or she may be consumed with cash flow, revenue growth, employees, and marketing which can take a lot of time and attention. So, this can mean giving someone the grace to deal with their professional engagements instead of feeling slighted. That can happen but remember, that's their livelihood.

But let's separate the genders. If you are dating a professional woman who has elevated herself in her world, consider the following. Women have worked hard and are very dedicated. They may have put forth a lot of effort to get to achieve a level of success. There are times when a woman may also feel she has to be perfect (because that what we do). She may have male counterparts who are not so pleased with her position. Equality can be tough in the working world and women have been surging and moving upward for the last four decades.

However, that doesn't mean that they don't want somebody in their life. Strong successful women want someone in their life to nurture them. A partner who can pamper them and baby them. A partner who they can have a good conversation with as well as good banter.

As a society, we judge successful and powerful women as aggressive, or even bitchy. In the last few decades, women have made strides in the professional world. Women feel a sense of responsibility to pave the way for other women.
Now let's move on to men. Men focus on one thing at a time. They do not multi-task well. When you are at the beginning stages of a relationship, he may be very attentive with calling and texting. However, as the relationship deepens that can change. Now you can feel neglected, slighted, or threatened.

When this occurs, the simple solution is to have a conversation. There could be something going on in the professional life that is consuming him. Always try to remain objective and do not lay any guilt or blame for lack of time. Do not tap dance around the issues and always have a direct conversation and lead with love.

Dating a man or woman in the professional world can be tricky and if you cannot deal with the amount of time they spend at their work or the lack of time with you, that is a decision you need to make. Objectively address the issue and try to refrain from talking when one of you is tired or inebriated. Maybe you need to set boundaries and make sure you both are spending good quality time together. No matter how long the discussion lasts, put your electronics away, and make the commitment to be present. When doing so both of you will experience greater emotional attachment. Always address issues while they are fresh because that may change, level out, and regulate the outcome of issues.

On the other side if you are the professional or owner of a business do not always assume everything is on your time. You need to be flexible as well. Don't disregard your partner's schedule because he or she may not be as busy as you. Be mindful that your partner has a life apart from yours. When you both are planning to spend quality time together, remember to take off your professional hat. When you're in a relationship changing your professional persona to a person can be difficult at times. For example, if you're a drill sergeant, or maybe a police officer, the temptation to bark orders is unconscious. Remember that you cannot be talking to your mate, as if you are ordering them around. Maybe you have a very demanding profession that takes you into boardrooms and into large groups of people where you have to sometimes be firm and strong with your words – while dating, make sure you listen to your tone and inflection and choice of words when you are with your partner.

When you are around somebody with whom you're building a relationship, recognize this is a journey and you are both trying to have an ever-lasting relationship with each other. Also always remember to check-in. You need to have benchmarks, and you need to ask each other, "How are you doing?" It would be great to check-in every couple of weeks and observe each other.

I have a dear friend whose daughter Melissa is a family marriage therapist. Melissa tells her clients to say to their partner, "Please rate me on how I'm doing as a husband or as a wife. On a scale of one to 10." You should do the same thing when you're dating somebody. Remember that at the end of the day, we're all made to have a connection. We're all made to want to be with somebody. Made to want to be cherished to want to be loved to want to be admired or want to be adored. And that's when you need to take the time and check-in with each other, to make sure you both are on the same journey together. Sometimes we veer off or have a detour. But that's okay - give each other a pass, try to focus on also making your relationship a priority. In the long run, and as the relationship gains more momentum and times passes, both of you will be able to meld into each other's lives together and work around whatever schedules the both of you have. You will both be on the journey of now being a Plus One!

BOOMERS ADOLESCENCE

Boomers Adolescence is a phrase that I coined when I personally started the dating process. I launched my profile like so many other people. I got more likes than I expected. I was excited, elated, even giddy. At times I was euphoric. I enjoyed the approval of others. Wait - I was inadvertently seeking the approval of others through social media. It was like being a teenager all over again. There I was. A successful businesswoman and, I was acting like a teenager. It felt great until I realized just how childish I was being. I had regressed. As I stopped and looked around, I found that many people in my age group were doing the same thing. They were baby boomers acting like teenagers. That's how the term Boomers Adolescence was created.

Boomers Adolescence is the period when adults find themselves acting and feeling like they are teenagers. I used the term boomer because the baby boomer generation is the group in which I see this most often. I also happen to be a baby boomer. Boomers adolescence is not completely negative. There can be several positives. If you're experiencing Boomers Adolescence you may be feeling fantastic. You may be feeling youthful. You might feel excited about life for the first time in a very long time. You may even feel energized strong and deeply connected to your emotions. You may feel like you're living again. These are the positive feelings that you may experience during this period of Boomers Adolescence. If you're over 50 years and you feel awakened, empowered, and youthful again then you're experiencing some of the wonderful benefits of Boomers Adolescence.

Now let's talk about some of the negative aspects of Boomers Adolescence. Impatient, impulsive, clingy, melodramatic. Do these sound like descriptions of a teenager or a mature adult? Well honestly, it depends. Teenagers are often described in such a way because they are often acting impulsively and making poor decisions. Impulsive behavior and poor decision-making can lead you to some very precarious situations. When you're a mature adult those situations can have some embarrassing and serious consequences. Read the following stories to see what it looks like when someone is experiencing Boomers Adolescence.

Mark was over fifty when he met a girl named Rene. He liked her pictures and her online profile. He could not wait to meet her in person. Mark texted her not once but several times a day before they met. Guess what? Mark was a little too impatient. Rene was turned off by his constant texting. Rene thought Mark was needy and let him know it! Needless to say, Mark did not make a love connection with Rene. His lack of patience and boyish neediness was a real turn off. What may be cute behavior for a teenager may be embarrassing behavior for an adult. This is what happens so often. We begin to act like teenagers again. We start acting like kids again. Our hormones are raging, the dopamine kicks in, and we get giddy. You want to love and be loved back. It's understandable. Just be patient, especially when a relationship is just developing.

Another pitfall of Boomers Adolescence is the issue of impulsive behavior followed by fantasy. If you knew Katherine, you may have been surprised by her story. She was a successful executive and had found herself thrust back into the dating world after having been married for nearly 20 years. Katherine met a great guy named Sam. One the first date they broke a few of the major rules of dating and got intimate. They had sex on the first date. They both acted very impulsively. There was romance and attraction between them and they took action. Unfortunately, some expectations were not clearly communicated before they became intimate. Katherine was looking for a long-term partner. Sam was looking for a causal relationship. Katherine was not aware of Sam's expectations and Sam was not aware of hers. Because they were intimate, Katherine had a strong emotional attachment to Sam. She began to call Sam repeatedly and he wasn't very responsive. She felt like he was ignoring her and was putting her on the back burner. Eventually, Sam did agree to another date with Katherine. On the day of the second date, Sam canceled. He may have agreed to see her just to placate Katherine. Instead of recognizing this about Sam, Kathrine then began daydreaming about them being together. Forever. As you can imagine, together forever didn't happen. Katherine was devastated. She spent days agonizing about their relationship. She called me in tears. She was crying so hard she had a hard time speaking and vomited. She was in such an emotional frenzy that she vomited over a guy. How is that for an example of adolescent behavior? My advice is to slow down and stay focused on reality. Leave fantasy for the novelists. You'll be much happier! Take a deep breath. You found someone you like and someone you want to get to know better and maybe have a long-term relationship with; so don't act like a teenager!

Boomers Adolescence is a good reminder that you should not put all your eggs in one basket, as they say. You need to have other things in life to occupy your time. Not everyone you meet is going to feel the same way about you as you feel about them. That's okay. Accept that it takes time to create the relationship you want. Sometimes we fantasize about a relationship. We create a dream and have high expectations and then suddenly, unexpectedly, the relationship is over. Discipline your mind by not allowing your emotions to get out of hand.

Have you ever been involved in what you might consider being a one-sided relationship? What I recommend to clients who have experienced a one-sided relationship is to determine why you were so deeply attached to the person and the relationship. Why did you try to please that person? Then turn the table and imagine yourself on the other side looking at your relationship from the perspective of your partner. Do you want someone who is always clinging and trying to please you? Often this behavior occurs because someone is desperate for attention. What does that desperation say about that person? Are they insecure and not confident? Remember self-confidence is sexy. The more you focus on building self-confidence and self-esteem the sexier you will be to potential partners.

My late husband used to say the difference between a reaction and an action is hesitation. I agree with him. The next time Boomers Adolescence sets in and tries to take over your emotions, count backward from 20, and then take a deep breath. Take the time to ask yourself this question, "How are these feelings serving me?" Often you will find that your feelings are masking some irrational fear. In the end, you will not smother someone and you will develop a healthy relationship; Leaving those raging young hormones for the youngins.

As I continue to talk about Boomers Adolescence and as we experience life. We also go through a reverse process as we age, especially when we're out there dating again. Since, we've been out of the dating world for a while and it's been quite some time now. I've witnessed situations where we (myself, clients, and men that I've met) sometimes think from the waist down and not the waist up , which is ridiculous. What happens is, verbal vomiting occurs, which is sharing your previous experience in order to connect with someone and get them to like you.

Early on in one of my relationships, the gentleman was trying so hard to impress me. However, during one conversation he asked me, "Did you ever cheat on your husband?" I was surprised that he asked me such a question and I answered emphatically NO. I had committed to our relationship and I would not want to have that happen to me. I follow the Golden Rule: Do unto others as you would have done unto you. So, I turned it around on him and asked him if he ever cheated on his wife. I was flabbergasted when he shared that he had several affairs during his marriage with his 40-year old wife. A perfect example of verbal vomiting! Here I had just told him I'm the type of woman who wants to be with somebody who was monogamous. His admission was solid evidence that he was not monogamous. That was a deal-breaker for me, he will probably be in his seventies now. Sometimes it best not to share everything. Keep it in the vault. Speaking about keeping it in the vault, I had a client who exemplifies keeping something in the vault and trusting someone with your heart and your deep secrets.

Denise met Adam on-line. When they met in person, they enjoyed each other's company. They started to see each other several times a week. They were about six weeks into their relationship when one night, they were just having a great conversation. The kind of conversation where you feel a connection. You both are present in the conversation. They were talking about some past dating experiences. Adam was discussing that he had had a brief relationship with another woman before he met her. And one of the things he told his past girlfriend, is that his ex-wife, unfortunately, had been taken by somebody online and gave that person quite a bit of money. The girl that he was dating also had that happen to her. Now his ex-wife had asked him not to share her experience with anyone. Well, he didn't listen because he shared it with the girl he was dating. Interestingly enough, this bit him in the ass because the two women met. The girl he was dating reached out to the ex-wife and said, "Hey, I heard you had an incident online where you gave somebody money. I did, too." Needless to say, this caused a rift between the ex-wife and Adam. When Denise heard about this, even though she wasn't a party to it, she thought that if she shared something private with him, it would not remain private. When something's in the vault, it's in the vault. Verbal vomiting just to gain acceptance into someone else's life can cause a lot of drama. Sharing an experience with someone else does not give you the privilege to share the story with others. Again, this is another example of Boomers Adolescence. We can't wait to tell the next person something that we were told that we shouldn't share. We should know at this stage in life that there are times we need to act like adults and sharing gossip or another person's private information is not acceptable. Even when we meet somebody that we truly like. We need to sometimes control those emotions. I spend a considerable amount of time with clients talking about Boomers Adolescence and sharing too much information. Again, when your emotions just erupt and you feel like you want to share too much, ask yourself if you really need to share this. If you do, the person you told knows your story. You have heard the phrase, "They know that you know and what now?".

If you get the urge to be needy and want to call or text someone because they did not contact you back immediately, take a moment, take a deep breath. Walk around, do something for about 20 minutes, and then see how you feel. Remember, you don't want to react, you want to act. And you want to have a relationship with somebody that's not going to cause you to always be on guard or make you feel out of balance. To get balanced, push aside that Boomers Adolescence. You have to practice and I know it's difficult. Sometimes I had to reach into my M & M jar in my kitchen (I keep about three lbs. of this candy all-time) and take several handfuls. Just take a moment to focus and you will feel better and in control. When taking these steps and not allowing the urges to overcome your feelings, you'll be on a path to finding somebody in your life. When you do find someone, you will be on equal footing and you will have clarity with where you are in life and in that relationship.

When a person earns the right to hear about your past, it should happen after you both have spent quite a bit of time with each other. What will feel good is that you feel comfortable and feel as if that person is honest and credible. So shed the Boomers Adolescence. Seeking the approval of others can be dangerous for so many reasons because I'm not the only one speaking from experience, my past dates and clients affirm this too. It's as if we revert to those teenage years. We become insecure and act childish like we are 15 again.

BLENDING FAMILIES

As we live more and when we enter our 40s and above, it's more than likely we've had one marriage or two, or several relationships You may have children. You have friends and other families from your past relationships. So, what do you do when now you meet someone and they have a family? It adds layers upon layers upon layers.

I remember when I met my husband in 1977. Frank was 12 years older than me. He had two children from a previous marriage, Tracy and Aaron. That was a little difficult for me because I had never had children. I come from a divorced family and my dad remarried. When I was being raised, the dynamism in my dad's home for children was "Do what I say and don't do what I do". My mother, unfortunately, had Schizophrenia and never came out of postpartum depression. She was in and out of mental institutions until she passed away in 2007. My dad didn't have to co-parent, I will address that later in this chapter. Frank and his wife, however, co-parented. This was different and new to me. It was foreign. Much to my chagrin they still had a cordial relationship. And Frank's family had a good relationship with Frank's ex-wife Sandy which was unfamiliar. It was a learning process for me. However, walking into a new relationship, without ever having children was quite a different experience.

The first time I met Frank's children, along with his mom and her husband, was in Las Vegas about 6 months after Frank and I started a relationship. They were staying at the Castaway Hotel in Las Vegas. Tracy was 10 years old and Aaron was 8 years old. Frank introduced them to me at the hotel and his daughter looked at him and asked, "Who is SHE, Daddy?" I remember Frank saying to me that his daughter was in a reptilian mood. I was staring down at a 10-year-old and I was only 12 years older than she. All I could remember was thinking that our relationship would be a battle.

When entering someone's world and interacting with their children as well yours, won't be as you anticipated. Some of you may remember the movie, "Mine, Yours and Ours" with Lucille Ball and Henry Fonda. In this movie, Lucille Ball had 8 children and Henry Fonda had 10. They endured a calamity of events, but they held it together, kudos to the writers. However, in real life, there are challenges with blended families and you need to remind yourself that, the children are young so they need guidance and reassurance from all adults around, you need to consider this, especially if you are entering into a new relationship with such circumstances. You may have your own beliefs and opinions about how your new girlfriend or boyfriend is parenting, but keep that to yourself. If you never have had children, this can be tricky for us because we think children can be taught easily and will listen. What a fallacy - wait till you have your own. Only offer advice if it is asked for. Stepping in between a parent and a child can be tricky. It's tough, but it's best you take a backseat in this situation.

Speaking of the backseat, I recall when I met my mother-in-law and she informed me that she was happy her son and I, were getting married. However, she did emphasize that Sandy (Frank's ex-wife) was her daughter-in-law too. Well, I was quite taken aback by that remark. It was like a slap in my face!! I was married to her son. I should have been MORE important than his ex-wife. How selfish that response was! It took me many years to understand she meant that she wanted to keep her connection with her ex-daughter-in-law because of her grandchildren. When you meet somebody and they still have children at home, you need to sometimes give them the right of way. That's right; give them the right of way. Allow all those in the relationship to have access to others from the previous relationship without being disgruntled. When you allow things to be, everything flows better and less stress-ful for all.

Speaking of my late mother Mary, at the latter stages of her life, because I did not try to change Mary's mind about me or how I should be more important than her first daughter in law. We be-came very close and at the end of her life, she only remembered me. Her two sons, Frank and John were her world. She only remembered me. She told the people in the nursing home she only had a daugh-ter, named Maria. That was so heartfelt for me be-cause I kept the peace and did not try to coerce her. When she passed, my husband thanked me and I was admired more, by my husband because of what I had demonstrated... Believe me, I ate crow many times... But in the end, it's not who wins it's who gives the other grace.

Take a moment and put yourself in the chil-dren's shoes, especially if they're living at home. They have their own insecurities, and they're going through certain periods in their life where they're dealing with fitting in, being socially acceptable, and school work. When their parents meet some-body new, how does that work for the kids? They may feel they are going to be replaced. It's tough because when there is a divorce or death, every-one deals with the outcome. Usually, their parent is the person who focuses on them (the children). The children receive the bulk of attention. But now their parent has you in their life and that can be overwhelming for a child. So how do you deal with it? Well, first take a step back and remember that those children were in your new partner's life long before you and that they do have a responsibility to the children. There's always going to be a connection between parent and child. No matter how wonderful or how difficult the child is, a parent always loves their child no matter what. They might not always like their children, but they certainly do love them.

Another thought to keep in mind is that you're not just dealing with children, you might be dealing with an ex. And that's also something that could be a bone of contention. But you need to be able to work past that and remember that you and your new partner are together by choice. The past partner or ex is no longer in your new partner's life except for if they have a bond and that's usually children (sometimes it's animals as well). So you need to give them their space, and again, don't ever offer advice unless it's solicited. Always remember, even if your advice is solicited, you need to choose your words carefully.

I'll never forget how insecure my stepson must have been at eight years old but then again, I would have been the same way, too. We were going down to Lake Havasu (Frank, me, Tracy, and Aaron) to visit Frank's mom and stepdad. Aaron wasn't feeling well so he decided he wanted to sit in front with his father. I was appalled. I felt that was my place –

the front seat. Talk about taking a backseat. I could have acted childishly and caused a ruckus. But I acquiesced and gave Aaron the front seat. When we got to our destination, of course, his grandmother coddled him. She also coddled Frank. Again, I took a backseat. On the way home, Frank thanked me sincerely for being good support. I responded by telling him that, under the circumstances, it was the right thing to do. I could have caused a whole destructive scene and called his behavior out. Instead, I just kept my observations to myself.

This situation could have caused a huge fight between Frank and myself. It could have caused some uncomfortable moments for the kids. Was it worth it? No. So I kept my observations to myself. Try not to have any battles when it comes to children. Pick your battles where they have merit and you have some solid ground. You will win with the children. So, I say be Switzerland.

Now, this doesn't mean that you must always keep your feelings to yourself, but it means you do sometimes. Remember that the difference between an action and a reaction is a hesitation. There are times in relationships where both partners have children. In such circumstances, you need to just count to 10 and maybe not even address the situation until you've had time to digest and clear your mind. You have to remember what you say to somebody can impact them for the rest of their lives. This can be positive, but it also could be negative, so it's very important to again take a step back.

I learned that as a child because I have a step-mom too. As a matter of fact, she's still alive. And I'll never forget that even stepparents are very insecure (I know I am still a stepparent). When my late father remarried, I think his wife, Diane felt that there was a competition between my dad's children but there wasn't at all. We were looking for ways to fit in. And it's important to remember that all the moving parts of blended families just want to find their place and fit in. You just have to give them the opportunity to have that sense of place, and always feel welcomed, that's the most important thing.

If you meet somebody and their children are out of the house, this too can be complex. Sometimes children that are out of the home can be obstacles when you meet your partner, I'm speaking out of an experience because I have a daughter who is in her 30s. Particularly because they think they know it all. Sometimes they can look at somebody you're dating and maybe give you their subjective, not objective, viewpoint. Bear in mind that even older children feel a bit threatened because you're moving into their parent's space. And sometimes it can also cause some friction when there is a little bit of financial imbalance as well which can be very uncomfortable. It is important that when you meet somebody, you take much time to know more about them; vetting them properly. Do your homework. When you meet someone and you two are spending time together, ask them questions about their children and how much time they spend with their family. You want to be able to blend your family and their family. You need to allow all of the moving parts, which is the extended family, to come together. More importantly, address the financial aspects before the two of you decide to move in together. What are you going to do legally to protect both of you should something happen to one of you or both of you at the same time? Because you certainly do not want to create a world war. Have this talk early and often. Before you two decide to move in together or buy a place or get married, do not avoid the conversation. What if one of you dies? How do you want the situation to unravel, especially with blended families? Talk and also work with any of your financial or legal teams, too. If you don't have legal guidance take the time and spend the money. In the long run, it will be beneficial for ALL.

During your time together as you are creating this new relationship and expanding your families in time you will grow to appreciate them. As the children grow older, they, too, will become wiser and appreciate you. The beauty of all of this is you both will have your memories of your past before you both met. Now you are incorporating your blended family. One day you can look at a snapshot of all of you together with a big smile on your face and a burst of joy in your heart. You took action and found somebody that you love, who loves you back, who understands you and you understand them. But if there are children, you just don't get them and they get you, now you have added more value to your life more family. Priceless! So, the ending of YOURS, MINE AND OURS will be harmonious.

CONCLUSION

Congratulations! You've made it through the book. Unlike those old college textbooks that are gathering dust on your bookshelf at home, this book can serve as a survival guide that you can take into the dating world. As much information and learning as you gleaned from this book, you have also gleaned a great deal of insight into who you are and who you want to be within a committed relationship. Just like washing your hands, taking a shower, and brushing your teeth, the processes that you learned in the book will give you the most benefit when you do them consistently. The real magic happens when you find a partner who readily embraces the concepts of being, loving, and rocking themselves. Together you can rock each other's worlds. Together you can change your world and spread peace and love. Together you can change the world. Have Fun!

ABOUT THE AUTHOR

Maria Romano is the founder of True Love Knots, a program she created specifically to help those looking for love later in life. She is a licensed and ordained minister in the wedding capital of the world, Las Vegas, Nevada. She has performed over 3000 weddings for 10 years. Maria is also a resilient entrepreneur who started the world's first woman-owned rental car company at one of the largest airports in the world. She has many years of experience and relationship insights working with couples, to solve their most important relationship challenges. Maria's passion is to help people get back into the dating world and help them feel confident, more importantly, she knows how difficult starting over can be, considering her personal experience. She strongly believes love has no age limits. After being married to the love of her life for 33 years, her husband passed away and she suddenly went from the perfect plus one to just one, which was not an easy experience. For that reason, she authored this wonderful book which shares her experiences and knowledge to make it easier for people who find themselves in her position. Hence, empowering them to *Go from a Just One to a Plus One.*